I0018109

# The Ultimate macOS Survival Guide

*Tips, Tools, and Techniques for Everyday macOS Users*

By Ryan Nowack

# Introduction: Welcome to macOS – A New Era of Computing

In January 1984, an eager crowd gathered in the Flint Center auditorium in Cupertino, California. The air buzzed with anticipation. Onstage, Steve Jobs stood behind a table, a cloth draped over what looked like a small, beige box. He smiled—knowing he was about to unveil something that would change computing forever.

With a dramatic pause, he pulled back the cover and pressed a button. The screen flickered to life, and a mechanical yet friendly voice greeted the world:

"Hello, I am Macintosh."

The crowd erupted into applause. Some gasped. Others stood in awe. It was the first time a personal computer spoke to its users, ushering them into a new era of computing.

This wasn't just another computer—it was a statement. Apple wasn't just creating a machine for programmers and tech enthusiasts. The Macintosh was revolutionary: it introduced a graphical user interface, a mouse, and a design philosophy that made technology personal. For the first time, everyday people—artists, writers, musicians—could interact with a computer without needing to type cryptic commands.

And just ten days before that historic keynote, Apple had already signaled its arrival with one of the most unforgettable commercials of all time.

The Ad That Changed Everything

The screen is black. A pale, dystopian world fades into view. A faceless army marches in perfect sync. Cold. Oppressive. Silent.

Suddenly, a woman appears—a runner in bright red shorts, gripping a massive sledgehammer. She dodges guards and sprints toward a massive screen, where a stern figure drones on. Just before they can stop her, she swings the hammer over her head and hurls it straight at the screen. BOOM. The screen shatters.

"On January 24th, Apple Computer will introduce Macintosh. And you'll see why 1984 won't be like '1984'."

That commercial, directed by Ridley Scott, aired only once during the Super Bowl. But that was all it needed. The message was clear: Apple wasn't just launching a product—it was starting a revolution.

Why macOS Still Stands Apart

From that moment, the Macintosh — and later macOS — kept redefining how we interact with computers. Today, millions of users around the world swear by MacBooks, iMacs, and Mac Studios—not just because of their sleek designs but because of what macOS represents:

A smooth, intuitive experience that just works—no hunting through menus, no confusing settings.

A seamless ecosystem where Macs, iPhones, iPads, and Apple Watches work together effortlessly.

A focus on privacy and security, ensuring your data stays yours.

A creative powerhouse, built for designers, musicians, and filmmakers.

Whether you just unboxed your first Mac or switched from Windows, you're stepping into a legacy of innovation.

This book is your survival guide: a no-nonsense roadmap to mastering macOS without the headaches.

No unnecessary jargon. No deep dives into the Unix kernel. Just real-world, everyday knowledge that will make using your Mac effortless and enjoyable.

Let's dive in—your macOS journey starts now.

# Chapter 1: macOS Basics – Navigating Your Mac Like a Pro

So, you've got a Mac in front of you. Maybe this is your first time using one, or maybe you're switching from Windows and wondering, "Where is the Start Menu?"

Don't worry—you're not alone.

macOS is designed to be intuitive, but if you've spent years using Windows, the differences can be frustrating at first. This chapter will walk you through the fundamentals so you can navigate your Mac with confidence. By the end, you'll know exactly how to open apps, find your files, and use the essential tools without feeling lost.

Let's get started.

The Desktop: Your New Home Base

When you turn on your Mac, the first thing you see is the desktop. This is where you'll access your files, applications, and system controls.

Key Features of the Desktop

Menu Bar (Top of the Screen): The control center of macOS. It changes based on the application you're using and contains system controls like Wi-Fi, battery, and volume.

Dock (Bottom of the Screen): A quick-access launcher for your favorite applications, currently open programs, and the Trash (the macOS equivalent of the Windows Recycle Bin).

Finder (Smiley Face Icon in the Dock): Your file manager, where you organize and access your documents, downloads, and other files.

Desktop Icons: Unlike Windows, macOS doesn't clutter the desktop with icons by default, but you can add them if needed.

Right-click (or tap with two fingers on the trackpad) on the desktop to create a new folder, change your wallpaper, or organize files.

## The Dock – Your Quick-Access Toolbar

The Dock is the row of icons at the bottom of your screen. It functions similarly to the Windows Taskbar, but with a more streamlined design.

What You'll Find in the Dock

App Icons: Frequently used and currently open applications.

Finder: Your main file management tool.

Trash: Where deleted files go before they're permanently removed.

Customizing the Dock

To remove an application, drag its icon out of the Dock until it disappears.

To add an application, drag it from Finder or Launchpad into the Dock.

Open System Settings > Dock & Menu Bar to:

Adjust the Dock size.

Enable hiding so the Dock disappears when not in use.

Turn on or off the magnification effect when you hover over icons.

Hover over an icon in the Dock, and you'll notice it enlarges slightly. This is called Magnification, and it can be adjusted in the settings.

## Finder – The macOS Equivalent of File Explorer

If you're coming from Windows, you might be looking for the C: drive. macOS organizes files differently, and Finder is where you'll manage them.

To open Finder, click the smiley face icon in the Dock or press Command (⌘) + N.

Key Features of Finder

Sidebar (Left Side): Provides quick access to Downloads, Documents, iCloud Drive, and external drives.

Search Bar (Top Right): Helps you find files quickly by name or content.

View Options (Top of the Window): Lets you switch between list view, grid view, and column view.

Unlike Windows, macOS doesn't assign drive letters. Instead, your main storage is labeled Macintosh HD. Files are organized under folders like Documents, Downloads, and Applications rather than scattered across a drive.

If you need to quickly preview a file without opening it, press the Spacebar—a feature called Quick Look.


The Menu Bar – The Hidden Power of macOS

At the top of the screen, you'll see the Menu Bar. It changes based on the application you're using.

What's in the Menu Bar?

Apple Logo (Top Left): Click this for system settings, sleep, shutdown, and log-out options.

App-Specific Menus: Every application has its own menu bar, where you'll find options like File, Edit, and View.

System Controls (Top Right): Here, you'll find Wi-Fi, battery status, Bluetooth, date & time, and volume controls.

To check your system information, click Apple Logo > About This Mac. This will show you details about your Mac, including the processor, memory, and macOS version.


System Settings – Where You Control Everything

System Settings (previously called System Preferences) is the macOS equivalent of the Windows Control Panel.

To access it, click the Apple logo in the top left and select System Settings.

Important Settings to Know

Wi-Fi & Network: Connect to the internet and manage network settings.

Displays: Adjust screen brightness, resolution, and external monitor settings.

Sound: Control volume levels and audio input/output devices.

Users & Groups: Add new users and manage login settings.

Privacy & Security: Manage permissions for apps, passwords, and system security.

Use the search bar at the top of System Settings to quickly find specific options.


Spotlight Search – The Fastest Way to Find Anything

Instead of hunting through folders, you can find almost anything on your Mac using Spotlight Search.

Press Command (⌘) + Spacebar to open it.

What You Can Do with Spotlight

Find files and applications instantly.

Perform quick calculations (just type "45+67" and hit Enter).

Look up word definitions and Wikipedia articles.

Check the weather, sports scores, and other real-time information.

For example, try typing "calculator" into Spotlight. You don't even need to open the app—you can perform the calculation right there.

# Trackpad Gestures and Keyboard Shortcuts – The "Aha!" Moment for New Mac Users

MacBooks have some of the best trackpads available, and learning a few gestures will make navigating macOS much easier.

## Essential Trackpad Gestures

Two-Finger Scroll: Move up or down, just like on a smartphone.

Three-Finger Swipe Up: Opens Mission Control, which shows all open windows.

Three-Finger Swipe Left/Right: Switch between full-screen applications.

Pinch to Zoom: Works exactly like it does on a smartphone.

You can customize these gestures in System Settings > Trackpad.

## Must-Know Keyboard Shortcuts

Command (⌘) + Q: Quit an application.

Command (⌘) + W: Close a window.

Command (⌘) + Tab: Switch between open applications.

Command (⌘) + Spacebar: Open Spotlight Search.

Command (⌘) + Shift + 4: Take a screenshot of a specific area.

## Your macOS Journey Has Begun

At this point, you should feel comfortable moving around your Mac, opening apps, and finding files. You've taken the first step toward mastering macOS.

In the next chapter, we'll go over setting up your Mac properly—configuring iCloud, adjusting system settings, and making sure everything is working exactly how you want it.

# Chapter 2: Setting Up Your Mac – The First Steps

Now that you know your way around macOS, it's time to set up your Mac properly. If this is your first time using a Mac, you might be wondering:

Do I need an Apple ID?

What is iCloud, and should I use it?

Why does my trackpad feel different from Windows?

How do I transfer my files from my old computer?

This chapter will walk you through each step, ensuring your Mac is configured correctly from the start.

Initial Setup – Getting Started

When you turn on your Mac for the first time, you'll see the Setup Assistant—a series of guided steps to configure your system.

Step 1: Select Your Language and Region

This ensures your keyboard layout, date format, and system preferences are correct.

Step 2: Connect to Wi-Fi

Your Mac will need an internet connection to continue setup, sign in to your Apple ID, and check for updates.

Step 3: Create or Sign In with an Apple ID

An Apple ID is your account for everything Apple—just like a Google account for Android or a Microsoft account for Windows.

Why You Need an Apple ID:

iCloud Syncing: Access your photos, notes, and documents across all Apple devices.

App Store & Software Updates: Download applications and keep them up to date.

Find My Mac: Locate your Mac if it's lost or stolen.

iMessage & FaceTime: Communicate with other Apple users.

If You Already Have an Apple ID:

Sign in using your existing credentials.

If You Don't Have an Apple ID:

Tap Create New Apple ID and follow the prompts. You'll need an email address and a secure password.

You can skip this step for now, but many features require an Apple ID, so it's best to set one up now.

iCloud Basics – What It Does and How to Manage Storage

Now that you're signed in, let's talk about iCloud.

What is iCloud?

iCloud is Apple's cloud storage service. It automatically syncs files, photos, contacts, messages, and other data across all your Apple devices.

Should You Use iCloud?

✅ Yes, if you want automatic backups, device syncing, and access to files from anywhere.

✖ No, if you prefer to store everything locally and don't want to rely on cloud storage.

Managing iCloud Storage

Apple gives you 5GB of free iCloud storage, but you may need more if you plan to store photos, backups, and documents.

To check or upgrade your storage:

Open System Settings.

Click Apple ID (at the top).

Select iCloud to see what's being stored.

Click Manage Storage to upgrade if needed.

Common iCloud features:

iCloud Drive: Stores documents, notes, and app data.

iCloud Photos: Automatically backs up your pictures and videos.

Find My Mac: Protecting against theft and remote locking.

You can enable or disable these options based on your preference.

Must-Adjust Settings – Making Your Mac More Comfortable

Before you start using your Mac daily, let's tweak a few settings to make navigation easier.

Trackpad Gestures and Scroll Direction

If you're coming from Windows, the way your Mac's trackpad scrolls may feel backward.

By default, Natural Scrolling is enabled — meaning scrolling up moves the page down, like on a phone. If you prefer Windows-style scrolling:

Open System Settings.

Go to Trackpad > Scroll & Zoom.

Toggle off Natural Scrolling.

You can also customize other gestures here, such as swiping between apps and using three fingers to open Mission Control.

Adjusting Notifications

By default, macOS sends notifications for emails, messages, calendar events, and app updates. If this gets overwhelming:

Open System Settings.

Select Notifications.

Turn off notifications for apps you don't need.

You can also enable Do Not Disturb to silence notifications during work hours.

Software Updates – Keeping Your Mac Secure and Up to Date

Just like Windows, macOS receives regular updates for security, performance improvements, and new features.

To check for updates:

Open System Settings.

Click Software Update (under General).

If an update is available, click Update Now.

You can also enable Automatic Updates to install new updates in the background.

Updating your Mac ensures you get the latest security patches and system improvements.

Transferring Data – Moving Files from a Windows PC or Another Mac

If you're switching from another computer, you probably want to bring your files with you.

Option 1: Using iCloud Drive

If your files are already stored in OneDrive, Google Drive, or Dropbox, you can access them immediately on your Mac by logging into those services.

If you used iCloud on your previous device, everything should sync automatically.

Option 2: Using an External Hard Drive or USB Drive

Plug your external drive into your Mac.

Open Finder and locate the drive in the sidebar.

Drag and drop files onto your Mac.

macOS supports exFAT and FAT32 file systems. If your drive is formatted as NTFS (a Windows-only format), you may need third-party software to write files to it.

Option 3: Using Migration Assistant (Best for Moving from an Old Mac)

Apple's Migration Assistant transfers files, applications, and settings from another Mac or PC.

To use Migration Assistant:

Open System Settings > General > Migration Assistant.

Follow the on-screen instructions to transfer data from another Mac or PC.

If you're moving from Windows, you'll need to install Windows Migration Assistant on your old computer (available from Apple's website).


Your Mac is Now Ready to Go

By now, you've:

Set up your Apple ID and system preferences.

Enabled or disabled iCloud based on your needs.

Adjusted settings like trackpad scrolling and notifications.

Updated your Mac to the latest version.

Transferred files from your old computer.

With these steps complete, your Mac is fully set up and optimized for everyday use.

In the next chapter, we'll explore customizing macOS—how to personalize the interface, set up widgets, and make your Mac feel like your own.

## Chapter 3: Customizing macOS – Making Your Mac Feel Like Home

Now that your Mac is set up and ready to go, it's time to make it your own. Right now, it's like a new apartment with plain white walls, factory-default furniture, and an unfamiliar layout. You could leave it like that, but wouldn't it feel better if it actually reflected you?

That's what this chapter is about—personalizing macOS so it feels comfortable, familiar, and efficient. Whether you prefer a sleek minimalist setup or a colorful workspace full of widgets and shortcuts, macOS gives you plenty of customization options.

Step 1: Changing Your Wallpaper (Because That's the First Thing Everyone Does)

Before you even open an app, chances are you want to change that default macOS wallpaper. It's nice, sure—but you didn't buy a Mac just to stare at a mountain or abstract gradients forever.

How to Change Your Wallpaper

Click the Apple Menu (top left) and go to System Settings.

Select Wallpaper.

Choose from macOS's built-in options or click Add Photo to use your own.

Pro Tip: Use Dynamic Wallpapers

Some macOS wallpapers change based on the time of day—morning, afternoon, and evening. If you want a subtle but cool effect, try one of these.

Step 2: Organizing the Dock – Stop the Clutter

The Dock is like your desk—it can be a clean, efficient workspace, or it can be an overflowing mess of apps you never use. Let's fix that.

Customizing the Dock

Right-click on any app in the Dock and select Remove from Dock if you don't use it often.

Drag your most-used apps (like Safari, Mail, or Notes) into the Dock for easy access.

Open System Settings > Dock & Menu Bar to:

Adjust the Dock size.

Enable hiding so the Dock disappears when not in use.

Turn on or off the magnification effect when you hover over icons.

Step 3: Enabling Dark Mode (Because It Looks Cool and Saves Your Eyes)

Dark Mode isn't just a trend—it's easier on your eyes, especially if you use your Mac late at night.

How to Enable Dark Mode

Open System Settings.

Go to Appearance.

Choose Dark Mode (or select Auto to switch based on the time of day).

You'll immediately notice macOS looking sleeker, with dark grays replacing bright whites. It's a small change, but for some users, it makes everything feel better.

## Step 4: Setting Up Widgets (Like a Personal Dashboard)

Widgets are small, helpful displays that show information at a glance—weather, calendar events, reminders, and more. They live in the Notification Center, which you can open by clicking the time in the top right corner.

### How to Add Widgets

Click the time in the Menu Bar (top right).

Scroll down and click Edit Widgets.

Drag widgets onto the panel to add them.

### Useful Widgets to Consider

Weather: Always know if it's sweater weather.

Calendar: See your upcoming events.

Reminders: A simple to-do list built into macOS.

Battery: If you use a MacBook, this helps track battery health.

## Step 5: Customizing System Sounds (If You Miss the Windows Startup Chime)

macOS has its own unique sounds, from the classic "pop" when you adjust volume to the soft chime when you start your Mac.

But did you know Apple removed the startup chime for a while? They brought it back after users complained—it turns out people like hearing a friendly boop when their Mac boots up.

### How to Adjust System Sounds

Open System Settings.

Go to Sound.

Adjust alert sounds, volume levels, and whether you want the startup chime enabled.

If you want to keep your Mac quiet, you can mute system sounds entirely.

## Step 6: Adjusting Trackpad & Mouse Settings (So It Feels Right to You)

If you've been using a Mac for a few hours and something feels off about the way the trackpad works, it's probably Natural Scrolling.

Apple assumes you want to scroll like an iPhone—moving up scrolls down, and down scrolls up. If that feels wrong:

How to Change Trackpad or Mouse Scrolling Direction

Open System Settings.

Go to Trackpad or Mouse.

Toggle off Natural Scrolling.

This will make scrolling feel like Windows, which many users prefer.

## Step 7: Setting Up Hot Corners (Mac's Best-Kept Secret)

Hot Corners let you trigger actions by moving your mouse to a corner of the screen.

How to Set Up Hot Corners

Open System Settings.

Go to Desktop & Dock > Hot Corners.

Assign actions to different corners, such as:

Show the Desktop.

Activate Mission Control (shows all open windows).

Put the Mac to Sleep instantly.

It takes a little getting used to, but once you master Hot Corners, they save time.

A Wild Story: The Case of the "Vanishing" Files

Everyone has that moment of panic when a file seems to disappear.

A client of mine—let's call him Mark—once spent an entire afternoon writing a report on his Mac. He swore he saved it to his desktop, but when he went back to find it—gone. Nowhere. Vanished.

Cue 20 minutes of frantic searching, retracing steps, checking the Downloads folder, even blaming his cat for walking across the keyboard.

Turns out? Spotlight Search had the answer all along.

One quick Command (⌘) + Spacebar, typing "report," and there it was—sitting safely in his Documents folder the entire time.

Lesson learned:

If you can't find a file, Spotlight can.

Never trust your memory on where you saved something.

If all else fails, check the Trash—you'd be surprised how often things end up there.

Your Mac, Your Way

At this point, you've:

Set a new wallpaper to personalize your Mac.

Organized the Dock so only useful apps are there.

Enabled Dark Mode for a sleeker look.

Added widgets to check important info at a glance.

Adjusted trackpad scrolling to match your preference.

Set up Hot Corners for quick actions.

Your Mac no longer feels like a factory-fresh machine—it feels like yours.

In the next chapter, we'll discuss one of the biggest hurdles for new Mac users: How macOS is different from Windows, and how to transition smoothly without frustration.

## Chapter 4: macOS vs. Windows – A Smooth Transition

So, you've been a Windows user for years, and now you're staring at your Mac thinking, "Where's the Start Menu? Where are my drives? How do I close apps?"

You're not alone.

Switching from Windows to macOS is like moving from driving an automatic car to a manual one. Both will get you where you need to go, but the controls feel different. At first, you might reach for something that isn't there, but once you get the hang of it, you'll wonder why you ever worried in the first place.

This chapter will guide you through the biggest differences between macOS and Windows so you can make the switch without frustration.

1. The Finder vs. File Explorer – Where Are My Files?

Windows users are used to opening File Explorer and navigating their folders under This PC or C:\ Drive. In macOS, this works differently.

Finder: The macOS File Manager

Instead of File Explorer, macOS has Finder, which you can open by clicking the smiley face icon in the Dock.

Here's what you'll see:

Sidebar (Left Side): Quick access to Documents, Downloads, iCloud Drive, and external drives.

Top Menu: Lets you change the file view (list, grid, or column view).

Search Bar: Located at the top-right for quickly finding files.

No C: Drive? Where Are My Files Stored?

On Windows, everything is under C:\Users\YourName.

 On macOS, your files live in Macintosh HD > Users > YourName.

Windows-style drive letters don't exist in macOS. Instead, your primary storage is called "Macintosh HD," and external drives just appear under "Locations" in Finder.

How to Open an External Drive:

Plug in a USB or external hard drive.

Open Finder and look under Locations.


2. Closing Apps – Why That "X" Button Works Differently

In Windows, clicking the X button in the corner of a window closes the application.

In macOS, clicking the red close button only closes the window, not the app itself. The app is still running in the background.

How to Fully Quit an App on macOS:

Use Command (⌘) + Q (the fastest way).

Right-click the app in the Dock and choose Quit.

Click the app's name in the Menu Bar (top left) and select Quit.

Why does macOS do this?

macOS assumes you might want to reopen the app quickly, so it keeps it running in the background unless you quit it manually.

3. The Start Menu vs. The Dock & Launchpad

Windows users rely on the Start Menu for launching programs. macOS doesn't have a Start Menu, but it offers two ways to open apps:

1. The Dock (For Quick Access)

The Dock at the bottom of the screen is like the Windows Taskbar. It holds frequently used applications and currently running apps.

Click an app icon to open it.

Right-click an app in the Dock to quit it or open recent files.

Drag an app into the Dock for easy access.

2. Launchpad (For All Apps, Like a Tablet)

If you want to see all installed applications, open Launchpad by clicking its icon in the Dock (it looks like a grid of squares) or pressing F4.

Launchpad is like an iPhone home screen. You can:

Click an app to open it.

Drag apps into folders for organization.

Search for apps using the search bar at the top.

If you prefer a Windows-style app list, you can also just use Spotlight Search (Command + Spacebar) and type the app's name.

4. Right-Clicking – The Mac Secret Every Windows User Needs to Know

On Windows, right-clicking is second nature. But when you try it on a Mac's trackpad, nothing happens.

That's because MacBooks don't have a physical right-click button—but the feature still exists.

How to Right-Click on macOS:

Two-Finger Tap (Default): Tap the trackpad with two fingers at once.

Control + Click: Hold the Control key while clicking.

Enable Right-Click Permanently:

Open System Settings.

Go to Trackpad > Secondary Click.

Choose Click with Two Fingers or Bottom-Right Corner Click (if you prefer a Windows feel).

5. Installing Apps – No EXE Files? What's a DMG?

Windows users download programs in .exe or .msi files. On macOS, apps usually come in .dmg or from the Mac App Store.

Installing Apps on macOS

If you download an app from the Mac App Store, installation is automatic.

If you download a .dmg file, follow these steps:

Open the .dmg file.

Drag the app into the Applications folder.

Eject the .dmg by dragging it to the Trash.

Uninstalling Apps on macOS:

Open Finder > Applications.

Drag the app to the Trash.

Empty the Trash to delete it permanently.

No "Uninstall Wizard" needed—just drag and drop.

## 6. Keyboard Shortcuts – The Windows Key vs. Command (⌘)

The Command (⌘) key on a Mac replaces the Control (Ctrl) key in Windows for most shortcuts.

Once you adjust to Command instead of Control, most shortcuts will feel familiar.

## 7. What About Viruses? Do I Need Antivirus Software?

On Windows, it's common to install antivirus software like Norton, McAfee, or Bitdefender.

On macOS, viruses are much less common, thanks to Apple's built-in security features:

Gatekeeper prevents untrusted apps from running.

XProtect automatically blocks known malware.

System Integrity Protection (SIP) stops unauthorized changes to system files.

Do You Need Antivirus?

For most users, no. But if you download apps outside the Mac App Store or visit risky websites, consider Malwarebytes for Mac for extra protection.

The Switch Gets Easier

Switching from Windows to macOS feels strange at first, but it doesn't take long to adapt.

By now, you know:

Finder replaces File Explorer for managing files.

The Dock and Launchpad replace the Start Menu.

Closing apps in macOS is different from Windows.

Right-clicking works with a two-finger tap.

Installing and uninstalling apps is simpler than on Windows.

The Command (⌘) key replaces Control (Ctrl) for shortcuts.

Once you stop expecting macOS to behave like Windows, you'll find it's just as easy to use—maybe even easier.

In the next chapter, we'll cover productivity shortcuts and tricks to help you work smarter on macOS.

## Chapter 5: Essential macOS Shortcuts and Productivity Tips – Work Smarter, Not Harder

Now that you're getting comfortable with macOS, it's time to unlock its full potential.

You've probably noticed that Macs are designed to be efficient, but many users—even those who've had a Mac for years—aren't aware of the hidden shortcuts and tools that can save time, boost productivity, and make everyday tasks easier.

This chapter isn't just about learning a few keyboard shortcuts. It's about working smarter, whether you're managing files, switching between apps, or trying to keep your hands off the mouse as much as possible.

By the end of this chapter, you'll be navigating macOS faster than ever.

1. Mastering the Keyboard – Essential Shortcuts You'll Actually Use

Most people know Command (⌘) + C for copy and Command (⌘) + V for paste. But macOS offers dozens of shortcuts that can cut seconds off every task—and those seconds add up.

Navigation Shortcuts (Forget the Mouse!)

Command (⌘) + Spacebar → Opens Spotlight Search (faster than Launchpad).

Command (⌘) + Tab → Switch between open applications.

Command (⌘) + W → Close the current window.

Command (⌘) + Q → Fully quit an application (not just close the window).

Command (⌘) + ` (backtick) → Switch between windows of the same app (great for Safari or Finder).

Command (⌘) + H → Hide the current application (keeps it open but out of sight).

Option + Click on Any App in the Dock → Instantly switches to that app and hides all others.

File & Text Shortcuts (Stop Dragging and Dropping!)

Command (⌘) + Shift + N → Creates a new folder in Finder.

Command (⌘) + Delete → Moves selected files straight to the Trash.

Command (⌘) + Shift + 3 → Takes a screenshot of the entire screen.

Command (⌘) + Shift + 4 → Lets you drag and select a specific area to screenshot.

Command (⌘) + Option + Esc → Opens the Force Quit menu to close unresponsive apps.

Bonus: Press Command (⌘) + Shift + T in Safari to reopen your last closed tab—a lifesaver if you close the wrong one by accident.

## 2. Spotlight Search – More Than Just a File Finder

Spotlight isn't just for searching files. It's one of the fastest ways to do almost anything on a Mac.

Press Command (⌘) + Spacebar and try these:

What Spotlight Can Do That You Probably Didn't Know

Math on the Fly: Type 74*25+10 and hit Enter—it calculates for you.

Unit Conversions: Type 10 miles in km or $50 in euros—no need to Google it.

Instant Dictionary Lookup: Type any word and see its definition instantly.

Quick App Launching: Type "Photos" or "Safari" instead of clicking icons.

Find Emails & Messages: Type a contact's name and see recent messages.

Search the Web Faster: Type a question (like "weather in New York") and hit Enter—it opens in Safari.

If you're not using Spotlight, you're wasting time digging through folders.

## 3. Mission Control & Spaces – How Mac Users Multitask Like a Pro

If you often find yourself buried in too many open windows, macOS has built-in tools to declutter your screen.

Mission Control (Your Mac's "Bird's Eye View")

Swipe up with three fingers on the trackpad (or press F3 on older Macs). This shows every open window so you can quickly switch between apps.

Spaces (Virtual Desktops – Organize Your Work)

Swipe left or right with three fingers to switch between multiple desktops.

Drag a window to the top of the screen in Mission Control to create a new desktop.

Use one desktop for work, one for personal browsing, and one for entertainment—no more messy overlapping windows.

Once you start using Spaces, you'll wonder how you ever worked without them.


4. Finder Power Tips – Managing Files Efficiently

Finder is more powerful than it looks. Here are a few tricks that even long-time Mac users don't always know:

Quick Look (Preview Any File Without Opening It)

Select a file and press the Spacebar—it shows a preview instantly.

Works with photos, PDFs, Word documents, and even videos.

Tag Your Files for Easy Organization

Right-click a file and add a color tag (Red for Important, Blue for Work, etc.).

In Finder, click the colored tags in the sidebar to quickly find files by category.

Batch Rename Multiple Files at Once

Select multiple files.

Right-click and choose Rename.

Rename them all sequentially or replace parts of the filenames.

This is great if you have 100 files named "IMG_001, IMG_002" and want them to be "Vacation_001, Vacation_002" instead.


5. Hidden Features You Didn't Know Existed

Macs have little-known features that can make life easier. Here are a few that most people don't discover on their own.

Use Your iPhone as a Scanner

Right-click on your desktop.

Select Import from iPhone > Scan Document.

Your iPhone will open its camera—take a picture, and it instantly appears on your Mac.

Copy & Paste Between Your Mac and iPhone (Universal Clipboard)

Copy text or an image on your iPhone.

Press Command (⌘) + V on your Mac—it pastes instantly.

Works the other way too! Copy something on your Mac and paste it on your iPhone.

Sign PDFs Instantly with Your Trackpad

Open a PDF in Preview.

Click the Markup Tool (Pen Icon).

Select Sign and use your trackpad to draw your signature.

Once saved, you can apply your signature with one click next time.

Hidden Emoji & Symbol Picker

Press Control + Command (⌘) + Spacebar anywhere to open the emoji & special character window.

No need to search through menus—just pop in a trademark symbol (™) or arrow (→) instantly.

A Story: The Case of the "Efficiency Overhaul"

A client of mine—we'll call him Tom—had been using a Mac for years but never knew about most of these features.

One day, he came to me frustrated about how slow he was at switching between windows and finding files. I showed him:

How to use Mission Control to organize his workspaces.

How to tag files in Finder for easy searching.

How to use Spotlight instead of clicking through menus.

The result?

Tom went from wasting minutes looking for files to finding them in seconds.

He stopped hunting through app icons and started launching apps instantly with Spotlight.

He never dragged a window manually again after learning keyboard shortcuts.

His response? "I feel like I've been using my Mac wrong this whole time."

You're Now a More Efficient Mac User

By now, you should be:

Navigating macOS faster with keyboard shortcuts.

Finding files instantly with Spotlight.

Managing multiple desktops with Mission Control.

Using Finder like a pro with Quick Look and tags.

In the next chapter, we'll tackle file management, storage solutions, and how to keep your Mac clutter-free.

## Chapter 6: Managing Files and Storage – Keeping Your Mac Organized

If you've ever spent 20 minutes looking for a file you swore you just saved—or if your desktop has become a graveyard of untitled documents and screenshots—you're not alone.

Everyone tells themselves, "I'll organize this later," but later never comes. Before you know it, your Mac's storage is full, Finder is a mess, and you're deleting old cat photos just to make space for new ones.

The good news? macOS has powerful built-in tools to keep your files organized—if you know how to use them.

This chapter will help you stop digging through folders, free up space, and keep your Mac clutter-free.

1. Where Do My Files Go? Understanding Finder and Storage Locations

The first step to staying organized is knowing where macOS puts your files.

Key Folders in macOS

Desktop: Everything you drag here stays visible—use it wisely.

Documents: Best for saving work files, PDFs, and written documents.

Downloads: The dumping ground for everything you download from the internet (clear this often!).

Applications: Where all installed apps live.

iCloud Drive: Apple's cloud storage for syncing files across devices.

Quick Tip: If your desktop is covered in random files, you can automatically organize them into stacks by right-clicking and selecting Use Stacks. This will group files by type (images, PDFs, screenshots, etc.), keeping things tidy.

## 2. Finder Tips That Will Save You Time

Finder is your file management tool, but most people only use it for the basics. Here are some tricks that will make organizing files much easier.

Use Tags for Instant File Sorting

Tags let you color-code files for quick access.

How to use them:

Right-click any file or folder.

Select a color tag (Red, Blue, Work, Important, etc.).

Click Tags in Finder's sidebar to instantly find related files.

Pin Favorite Folders for Quick Access

Open Finder and navigate to a folder you use often.

Drag it into the left sidebar under "Favorites"—now it's always one click away.

## 3. The Search Trick You Didn't Know About

Have you ever tried searching for a file but Finder just gives you a thousand results?

Here's a better way:

Open Finder and press Command (⌘) + F.

Use the dropdown menus to search by file type, date modified, or specific words inside documents.

For example, if you remember you worked on a contract last month but forgot the filename, set the search to:

Kind: Document

Last Opened: Within the Last 30 Days

Suddenly, that needle in the haystack becomes easy to find.


## 4. iCloud Drive vs. Local Storage – Where Should You Save Files?

macOS gives you two main storage options:

Option 1: iCloud Drive (Cloud Storage for Syncing Across Devices)

Keeps files backed up online.

Accessible on Mac, iPhone, iPad, and even Windows.

Prevents files from getting lost if your Mac crashes.

Option 2: Local Storage (Saved Only on Your Mac)

Good for large files (videos, high-resolution images).

Doesn't take up iCloud space.

Always accessible, even without the internet.

Quick Tip: If you have a smaller hard drive, turn on Optimize Mac Storage in System Settings > Apple ID > iCloud. This keeps recent files on your Mac but moves older ones to iCloud.


## 5. Clearing Space – What's Eating Up Your Storage?

One day, macOS will hit you with the dreaded "Your disk is almost full" warning—usually when you need space immediately.

Here's how to free up storage fast.

Find Out What's Taking Up Space

Open System Settings.

Click General > Storage.

You'll see a breakdown (Apps, Photos, Mail, System, etc.).

Now that you know what's hogging space, here's how to clean it up.

1. Empty Your Downloads Folder (The Black Hole of Storage)

Open Finder > Downloads.

Delete anything you don't need—this folder fills up fast.

2. Delete Large Files (Without Digging Through Folders)

Open Finder and press Command (⌘) + F.

Set the filter to File Size > Greater Than > 500MB.

Delete anything you don't need.

3. Use macOS's Built-In Storage Cleaner

Go to System Settings > General > Storage.

Click Review Files to remove unused apps, large files, and system clutter.

4. Empty the Trash (Yes, You Need to Do This)

Files in the Trash still take up space!

Right-click the Trash icon in the Dock and select Empty Trash.

## 6. External Drives and Backup – The Lifesaver You'll Wish You Had

If you have important files, you should back them up—because one day, something will go wrong.

Option 1: Use Time Machine (macOS's Built-in Backup Tool)

Plug in an external hard drive.

Open System Settings > Time Machine.

Select Back Up Automatically.

Time Machine keeps hourly, daily, and weekly backups, so if you accidentally delete a file, you can restore it with a few clicks.

Option 2: Use an External Hard Drive for Extra Storage

If your Mac's storage is full, an external drive is an easy solution.

Use exFAT format if you want to use the drive on both Mac and Windows.

If using it only on Mac, format it to APFS for faster performance.


A Story: The Case of the "Vanishing" Files

Everyone has that moment of panic when a file seems to disappear.

A client of mine—let's call him Mark—once spent an entire afternoon writing a report on his Mac. He swore he saved it to his desktop, but when he went back to find it—gone. Nowhere. Vanished.

Cue 20 minutes of frantic searching, retracing steps, checking the Downloads folder, even blaming his cat for walking across the keyboard.

Turns out? Spotlight Search had the answer all along.

One quick Command (⌘) + Spacebar, typing "report," and there it was—sitting safely in his Documents folder the entire time.

Lesson learned?

If you can't find a file, Spotlight can.

Never trust your memory on where you saved something.

If all else fails, check the Trash—you'd be surprised how often things end up there.


Now You're in Control of Your Files

Your Mac no longer feels like a black hole where files disappear. You now know:

Where macOS stores your files.

How to use Finder's best tools (tags, Quick Look, and Smart Search).

When to use iCloud Drive vs. local storage.

How to free up storage fast.

Why Time Machine is the easiest way to protect your files.

Next up? Must-have apps for productivity, creativity, and making macOS even better. Let's explore the best built-in and third-party apps to supercharge your Mac experience.


## Chapter 7: Must-Have Apps for macOS – The Best Tools (Without Breaking the Bank)

Your Mac is set up, organized, and running smoothly. Now, it's time to load it up with apps that make life easier.

But here's the thing: you don't need to spend hundreds of dollars on software to have a fully functional, powerful Mac.

When people switch to macOS, they often assume they need to buy Microsoft Office, Photoshop, a fancy video editor, and some overpriced "Mac Cleaner" app. The truth?

There are plenty of free or budget-friendly alternatives that work just as well—sometimes better.

In this chapter, we'll cover the best built-in macOS apps, free alternatives to paid software, and a few essential tools that every Mac user should know about.

A Story: The Case of the "Expensive Software Trap"

A client of mine—let's call him Jake—had just switched to a Mac. He was excited, but also a little overwhelmed.

"I just want to get everything set up properly," he told me.

A week later, he came back and proudly showed me his new apps.

Microsoft Office – $149

Adobe Photoshop – $21 per month

Final Cut Pro – $299

A Mac "cleaner" software – $49

Total spent? Over $500.

I had to break it to him gently: he didn't need to spend all that money.

LibreOffice does everything Microsoft Office does—for free.

GIMP is a free Photoshop alternative that works great for most users.

DaVinci Resolve is a professional-grade video editor—and it's free.

And that Mac cleaner app? Completely unnecessary—macOS already has built-in tools to clean up storage.

His reaction? "I wish I had known this before I spent all that money."

So consider this chapter your money-saving guide to essential Mac apps—so you don't fall into the same trap.

## 1. Great Built-In macOS Apps You Should Actually Use

Before downloading anything, let's talk about the apps your Mac already has.

Safari – The Browser That Saves Battery Life

Many people immediately install Chrome, but Safari is optimized for Macs and uses way less battery.

Faster than Chrome on MacBooks.

Blocks trackers and ads automatically.

Syncs seamlessly with iPhone and iPad.

Pro Tip: If you want to switch but are worried about losing your bookmarks and passwords:

Go to Safari > File > Import From > Google Chrome, and everything transfers over.

Preview – The Secret Powerhouse for PDFs

Most people just use Preview to open images, but it's actually one of the best free PDF tools out there.

Digitally sign documents using your trackpad—no printing required.

Merge multiple PDFs into one by dragging them into Preview.

Basic image editing (cropping, annotating, resizing) without needing Photoshop.

Notes – The Underrated Productivity Tool

Apple Notes looks simple, but it's way more powerful than most people realize.

Syncs across all Apple devices for free.

Supports checklists, drawings, and scanned documents.

Lets you lock notes with a password for extra privacy.

Pro Tip: Take a screenshot (Command (⌘) + Shift + 5), then drag it into Notes for instant reference.

## 2. The Best Free or Cheap macOS Apps for Productivity

Rectangle (Free) – The Window-Snapping Tool macOS Should Have Built-In

If you miss Windows' "snap to edges" feature, you need Rectangle. It lets you:

Snap windows to halves, corners, or full screen using simple shortcuts.

Quickly arrange multiple apps without dragging windows around.

How to Get It: Download for free at

LibreOffice (Free) – The Best Alternative to Microsoft Office

If you don't want to pay for Microsoft Office, LibreOffice is a free, full-featured alternative.

Opens and edits Word, Excel, and PowerPoint files.

No subscriptions—just download and use.

How to Get It: Download for free at

Amphetamine (Free) – Keeps Your Mac Awake When You Need It

Ever been in the middle of a long download or Zoom call and your Mac randomly goes to sleep?

Amphetamine keeps your Mac awake only when you need it—no more interruptions.

How to Get It: Search Amphetamine in the Mac App Store.

## 3. Best Free or Cheap Apps for File Management

### The Unarchiver (Free) – Open Any ZIP, RAR, or 7z File

macOS can unzip ZIP files, but it can't open RAR, 7z, or other formats—The Unarchiver can.

How to Get It: Search The Unarchiver in the Mac App Store.

### DaisyDisk ($9.99, One-Time Purchase) – Find Out What's Eating Your Storage

Shows a visual breakdown of what's taking up space.

Helps you delete large, unnecessary files quickly.

How to Get It: Visit

## 4. Best Free or Cheap Apps for Creativity

### GIMP (Free) – A Photoshop Alternative Without the Price Tag

Photoshop is expensive. GIMP is free, open-source, and does most of what Photoshop can do.

How to Get It: Download for free at

### DaVinci Resolve (Free) – A Hollywood-Grade Video Editor for $0

Used by professional video editors, but the free version is powerful enough for everyday users.

How to Get It: Download for free at blackmagicdesign.com

## 5. Small Utilities That Make a Big Difference

HiddenMe (Free) – Instantly Hide Desktop Icons for a Clean Look

Perfect for presentations or recording your screen.

How to Get It: Search HiddenMe in the Mac App Store.

Itsycal (Free) – A Menu Bar Calendar (Because macOS Doesn't Have One!)

If you miss the clickable calendar in Windows, this adds it to macOS.

How to Get It: Download for free at mowglii.com/itsycal

Now You Have Everything You Need—Without Overspending

With these apps, your Mac is now:

✓ More productive with better window management and office tools.

✓ Better at managing files and storage.

✓ Loaded with powerful creative tools—for free or cheap.

Next up? Staying safe online. In the next chapter, we'll cover browser security, privacy settings, and how to avoid common internet scams.

## Chapter 8: Browsing and Internet Security – Staying Safe Online Without the Paranoia

The internet is a wild place.

From sketchy pop-ups claiming you've won an iPhone to emails demanding you reset your password for an account you don't even have, there's no shortage of scams, viruses, and data trackers trying to get into your business.

Luckily, macOS is one of the most secure operating systems out there—but that doesn't mean you're invincible.

A lot of people assume, "Macs don't get viruses." While it's true that macOS is far less targeted than Windows, it's not completely immune to online threats. Scams, phishing emails, and sneaky malware still exist, and the more you know, the safer you'll be.

This chapter will teach you how to browse safely, protect your data, and avoid common online traps—all without installing expensive security software.

1. The Myth: "Macs Don't Get Viruses"

Let's clear this up right away:

Macs can get malware (but it's much less common than on Windows).

Macs don't need antivirus software (if you follow safe browsing practices).

Apple already has built-in protections against most threats.

Interesting Fact: Macs Have a Built-in Antivirus That Most People Don't Know About

Did you know that macOS already has a hidden antivirus system running in the background?

It's called XProtect, and it works like Windows Defender—but silently.

XProtect automatically scans every app you open and blocks anything suspicious.

It updates in the background, so you're always protected.

Unlike paid antivirus software, it doesn't slow down your Mac.

That's why most Mac users never see a virus warning—XProtect quietly handles threats before you even notice them.

That said, XProtect won't save you from phishing scams or bad browsing habits, which brings us to…

## 2. Safe Browsing: How to Avoid Internet Traps

### Safari vs. Chrome: Which Browser Should You Use?

Most Mac users immediately install Google Chrome—but is that the best choice?

Safari is optimized for macOS, so if you care about battery life and privacy, stick with Safari.

That said, Chrome is still useful if you rely on Google services or need certain extensions.

Pro Tip: If you use Chrome but want better privacy, go to Settings > Privacy and Security > Send "Do Not Track" requests to limit data collection.

### How to Spot (and Avoid) Fake Websites

Scammers love creating fake versions of real websites to steal passwords and credit card details.

Before entering your login info anywhere, check for these red flags:

▶ The URL looks slightly wrong (like "amaz0n.com" instead of "amazon.com").

▶ The site demands urgent action ("Your account will be locked in 24 hours!").

▶ It asks for personal information too quickly (real sites don't ask for credit card info upfront).

Pro Tip: If a site looks suspicious, don't click anything—just type the URL manually into your browser.

### The Pop-Up Scam That Tricks Millions Every Year

Ever seen a pop-up saying "Your Mac is infected! Click here to clean it"?

It's a scam. Your Mac does not need a cleaner app.

These pop-ups try to trick you into downloading fake antivirus software that actually infects your computer. If you see one:

Don't click anything.

Close the tab or quit the browser.

If it won't close, force quit using Command (⌘) + Option + Esc.


## 3. Password Security: One Simple Trick to Keep Your Accounts Safe

Stop Using the Same Password for Everything

Most data breaches happen because people reuse passwords across multiple accounts. If a hacker gets one, they can get into all of them.

Solution? Use a password manager.

macOS already has one built-in:

Open System Settings > Passwords to view, edit, and generate secure passwords.

Safari will auto-fill passwords for you, so you don't have to remember them.

If you need a third-party option, Bitwarden (free) or 1Password (paid) are great choices.


Turn on Two-Factor Authentication (2FA)

Even if someone steals your password, 2FA blocks them from logging in.

Enable it for bank accounts, emails, and social media.

Use an authenticator app (Google Authenticator, Authy) instead of SMS if possible.


## 4. Should You Install Antivirus on a Mac?

If you follow safe browsing practices, you don't need an antivirus. However, if you:

✅ Download software from random websites.

✅ Share files with Windows users (Macs don't get Windows viruses, but they can spread them).

✅ Want an extra layer of protection…

Then Malwarebytes Free is a solid, lightweight option for scanning your Mac if you suspect something's wrong.

What You Don't Need: Expensive antivirus subscriptions like McAfee or Norton—they often slow down your Mac and aren't necessary.

5. Public Wi-Fi Safety – Avoid Getting Hacked at Coffee Shops

Public Wi-Fi is not safe—hackers can intercept your connection and steal your data.

How to Stay Safe on Public Wi-Fi

✅ Avoid logging into banking or sensitive accounts on public networks.

✅ Use a VPN like ProtonVPN (free) to encrypt your connection.

✅ Turn off AirDrop in System Settings > General > AirDrop & Handoff to prevent strangers from sending files to you.

A Story: The Case of the "Accidental Hacker"

A client of mine—let's call him Jake—was messing around on his laptop one night when he suddenly got locked out of his own bank account. He hadn't forgotten his password, and nobody else had access to his computer. Confused, he called the bank.

"Sir, we detected suspicious login attempts from multiple locations. Your account was locked for security reasons."

Jake panicked. Had he been hacked?

Nope. He had been hacked… by himself.

Here's what happened:

Earlier that week, he reused the same password for a random website.

That website got hacked and leaked his password.

Hackers tried logging into his bank account using that leaked password.

His bank locked him out before the hackers could steal his money.

Jake had no idea that using the same password on multiple sites was dangerous. If his bank hadn't caught it in time, he could have lost everything.

Final Thoughts: Stay Smart, Stay Safe

By now, you know how to:

Use strong passwords and a password manager.

Turn on two-factor authentication for extra protection.

Recognize phishing scams before they trick you.

Stay safe on public Wi-Fi with simple precautions.

Next up? Troubleshooting common macOS issues. Whether it's a slow Mac, Wi-Fi problems, or apps freezing, the next chapter will show you how to fix the most common Mac headaches—without calling tech support.

# Chapter 9: Troubleshooting Common Issues – Fix Problems Fast Without Calling Tech Support

Even the best computers run into problems from time to time. Maybe your Mac suddenly starts running slow, Wi-Fi stops working, or an app won't open no matter what you do.

You might be wondering, "Is it time for an upgrade?"

Not so fast! Most Mac issues are easy to fix—if you know where to look.

This chapter will walk you through the most common macOS problems and their solutions—step by step, in plain English. By the end, you'll feel confident solving issues yourself, without wasting hours searching for answers or calling tech support.

1. Mac Running Slow? Here's How to Speed It Up

A slow Mac can make even the simplest tasks painfully frustrating. But before you start Googling "Why is my Mac so slow?", try these fixes.

Step 1: Restart Your Mac (Yes, Really!)

It sounds obvious, but many people never restart their computers. macOS is designed to run efficiently without needing frequent restarts, but too many apps running for too long can slow things down.

Click the Apple menu (top left) > Restart.

If an app is frozen and won't let you restart, press Command (⌘) + Option + Esc to force quit it first.

Step 2: Check If You're Running Out of Storage

A nearly full hard drive can slow your Mac to a crawl.

Open System Settings > General > Storage.

If you have less than 10GB of free space, delete large files or move them to an external drive.

Step 3: Close Background Apps You Don't Need

Some apps keep running even after you close their windows.

Open Activity Monitor (Finder > Applications > Utilities).

Click the CPU tab to see which apps are using the most resources.

If something looks suspiciously high, click it and select Quit Process.

💡 Pro Tip: If your MacBook gets hot or the fan is always running, check for Google Chrome in Activity Monitor—Chrome is a known resource hog.

2. Wi-Fi Not Working? Try This First

If your Mac's Wi-Fi stops working, don't panic. Try these steps before calling your internet provider.

Step 1: Turn Wi-Fi Off and On Again

Click the Wi-Fi icon in the menu bar and toggle it off. Wait 10 seconds, then turn it back on.

Step 2: Restart Your Router

Unplug your router for 30 seconds, then plug it back in. This fixes more internet problems than you'd think.

Step 3: Forget the Network and Reconnect

If your Wi-Fi is still acting up:

Open System Settings > Wi-Fi.

Click your Wi-Fi network and select Forget This Network.

Reconnect by selecting it again and entering the password.

Step 4: Check If Your Mac's Wi-Fi Is the Problem

If other devices (phones, tablets, another computer) are also losing Wi-Fi, the issue is likely your internet provider, not your Mac.

If only your Mac has issues, try resetting your Network Settings:

Open System Settings > Network.

Click the three dots (…) and select Reset Network Settings.

💡 Still No Luck? Connect your Mac directly to the router using an Ethernet cable. If the wired internet works, you might need a new router.

3. Apps Keep Freezing or Crashing? Here's the Fix

Few things are more annoying than an app freezing right when you need it. If an app won't open, keeps crashing, or is stuck, try this:

Step 1: Force Quit and Restart the App

Press Command (⌘) + Option + Esc to open the Force Quit menu.

Select the frozen app and click Force Quit.

Restart the app and see if it works.

Step 2: Update the App

Open the App Store and go to Updates.

If the app is from the web, check the developer's website for updates.

Step 3: Delete and Reinstall the App

If an app refuses to work, delete it and reinstall it.

Open Finder > Applications.

Drag the app to the Trash, then reinstall it from the Mac App Store or the original website.

## 4. Mac Won't Turn On? Try These Steps Before Panicking

If your Mac refuses to start, it could be something simple. Try these basic troubleshooting steps before assuming the worst.

### Step 1: Check the Power

If you're on a MacBook, make sure it's plugged in and the charger is working.

Try a different outlet or a different charging cable.

### Step 2: Force Restart Your Mac

Press and hold the power button for 10 seconds, then let go and press it again.

### Step 3: Reset the NVRAM & SMC (Advanced Users Only)

If your Mac still won't start, try resetting the NVRAM (a small memory that stores settings).

Turn off your Mac.

Press and hold Option + Command (⌘) + P + R for 20 seconds while turning it on.

For MacBooks, you may also need to reset the SMC (System Management Controller):

Turn off your Mac.

Hold Shift + Control + Option and press the power button for 10 seconds.

If none of these steps work, your battery or hardware might need repair.

## 5. External Devices Not Working? Fix USB, Printers, and Hard Drives

USB Device Not Recognized? Try This:

Unplug it and plug it into a different USB port.

Restart your Mac.

If it's a flash drive or external hard drive, check Finder > Locations—it may just need to be manually mounted.

Printer Won't Print? Try This:

Open System Settings > Printers & Scanners.

Click your printer and select Remove Printer.

Re-add it by clicking Add Printer and following the steps.

💡 Still not working? Check if your printer needs new drivers from the manufacturer's website.

Final Thoughts: Now You Can Fix Common Mac Problems Yourself

By now, you've learned how to:

Speed up a slow Mac by closing background apps and freeing up storage.

Fix Wi-Fi issues by resetting your network and router.

Troubleshoot frozen apps with Force Quit, updates, and reinstalls.

Deal with a Mac that won't turn on by checking power connections and resetting NVRAM/SMC.

Solve external device issues by re-adding printers and checking USB drives.

Instead of panicking the next time something goes wrong, you'll know exactly what to do—no tech support call required.

Up next? Optimizing macOS performance—how to keep your Mac running smoothly and efficiently for the long haul.

## Chapter 10: Optimizing macOS Performance – Keep Your Mac Running Like New

At first, your Mac runs like a dream—fast, smooth, and effortless. But over time, things start to slow down. Apps take longer to open, the spinning beach ball appears more often, and your once-speedy machine starts feeling sluggish.

You might be wondering, "Is it time for an upgrade?"

Not so fast! Before you even think about spending money on a new Mac, there are simple ways to boost performance and make your current machine run like new.

In this chapter, we'll cover how to clean up your system, reduce background clutter, and keep your Mac running efficiently—all without buying anything or installing shady "Mac cleaning" software.

A Relatable Story: The "Slow Mac Panic" That Wasn't

A friend of mine—let's call her Lisa—came to me in full panic mode.

"I think my Mac is dying," she said, "It's taking forever to open apps, the fan is running like crazy, and I can't even switch between windows without lag."

She was convinced she needed to buy a brand-new Mac. But after just 10 minutes of troubleshooting, we found the problem.

She had 50+ tabs open in Chrome.

Her storage was almost full.

She hadn't restarted her Mac in three months.

We closed unnecessary tabs, cleared some space, restarted her Mac, and—boom—her Mac was running fast again.

This happens all the time. Many people assume their computer is broken when really, it just needs some basic maintenance.

So before you start shopping for a new Mac, try these simple steps first.

1. Free Up Storage Space (Because a Full Hard Drive Slows Everything Down)

If your Mac's storage is almost full, your system will slow down—this is because macOS needs extra space to run efficiently.

Check Your Storage

Open System Settings > General > Storage.

Look at what's taking up the most space (Applications, Documents, Photos, etc.).

If you have less than 10GB free, you need to clear some space.

How to Quickly Free Up Space

✓ Delete Large, Unused Files:

Open Finder, press Command (⌘) + F, and set File Size > Greater than > 500MB.

Delete anything you don't need.

✓ Empty the Trash:

Right-click the Trash in the Dock and select Empty Trash.

✓ Clear Out Downloads:

Open Finder > Downloads and delete old files you don't need.

✓ Use iCloud for Storage:

Open System Settings > Apple ID > iCloud.

Enable Optimize Mac Storage to automatically move older files to iCloud.

💡 Quick Tip: If you have a lot of photos or videos, move them to an external hard drive instead of storing them on your Mac.

## 2. Reduce Startup Programs (Stop Unnecessary Apps from Slowing Down Your Boot Time)

If your Mac takes forever to start up, it's probably because too many apps are launching automatically.

How to Disable Startup Apps

Open System Settings > General > Login Items.

Look at the list of apps that open at startup.

Remove anything unnecessary by selecting it and clicking the minus (-) button.

Common offenders? Spotify, Zoom, Adobe apps, and messaging apps—if you don't need them at startup, disable them.

## 3. Close Background Apps That Use Too Many Resources

Some apps keep running in the background, even when you're not using them.

How to See What's Slowing Down Your Mac

Open Activity Monitor (Finder > Applications > Utilities).

Click the CPU tab and look for apps using a high percentage.

Select any unnecessary app and click Quit Process.

💡 Pro Tip: If your MacBook gets hot or the fan is always running, check for Google Chrome in Activity Monitor—Chrome is a known resource hog.

## 4. Restart Your Mac Regularly (Seriously, Just Do It)

If you haven't restarted your Mac in weeks or months, it's probably running slower than it should.

Restarting clears memory, refreshes the system, and fixes small bugs.

Aim to restart at least once a week for best performance.

To restart: Click the Apple menu > Restart.

## 5. Keep Your macOS and Apps Updated

Software updates aren't just about new features—they also fix bugs and improve performance.

How to Check for macOS Updates

Open System Settings > General > Software Update.

If an update is available, install it.

Update Your Apps Too

Open the App Store, go to Updates, and install any pending updates.

If you have apps installed from outside the App Store, check the developer's website for updates.

## 6. Manage Your Browser Tabs (Because Too Many Can Kill Performance)

Web browsers, especially Google Chrome, can drain your Mac's memory and slow everything down.

How to Prevent Browser Slowdowns

✅ Limit open tabs – Close any tabs you're not actively using.

✅ Use Safari instead of Chrome – It's more efficient on macOS.

✅ Try an ad blocker – Ads can slow down pages and eat memory.

💡 Tip: If you must use Chrome, install The Great Suspender extension to automatically pause unused tabs.

## 7. Reset Your System Settings If All Else Fails

If your Mac still feels slow, it might be time for a fresh start.

How to Reset System Settings (Without Losing Your Files)

Open System Settings > General > Transfer or Reset.

Click Erase All Content and Settings (this won't delete your files, just system settings).

Follow the prompts to reset your Mac's settings without erasing personal data.

💡 Warning: This should be a last resort—only do it if nothing else works.

## Final Thoughts: Keep Your Mac Running Like New

Lisa was ready to buy a new Mac because she thought hers was broken. But all she needed to do was:

Close background apps and excessive Chrome tabs.

Free up storage by clearing out old files.

Restart her Mac (something she hadn't done in months).

Her Mac went from painfully slow to running smoothly in just 20 minutes.

And now, you know how to do the same.

By following these simple steps, your Mac will stay fast, efficient, and frustration-free—without spending a dime.

Next up? Security and privacy—how to lock down your Mac and protect your personal data from hackers, trackers, and nosy apps. Let's talk about how to keep your data safe and stay in control of your privacy.

## Chapter 11: Security and Privacy on macOS – Keeping Your Data Safe Without Losing Your Mind

These days, privacy is a big deal. Every website, app, and tech company seems to want a piece of your personal information. Your Mac may be secure, but are you?

Maybe you're thinking, "I don't have anything to hide." But security isn't just about hiding things—it's about protecting your personal info from hackers, scammers, and companies that track you for profit.

Your Mac has excellent built-in security features—but most people don't use them. This chapter will show you how to lock down your Mac, secure your accounts, and browse the internet safely—without making things complicated.

A Wild Story: The Case of the "Accidental Hacker"

A client of mine—we'll call him Jake—was messing around on his laptop one night when he suddenly got locked out of his own bank account. He hadn't forgotten his password, and nobody else had access to his computer. Confused, he called the bank.

"Sir, we detected suspicious login attempts from multiple locations. Your account was locked for security reasons."

Jake panicked. Had he been hacked?

Nope. He had been hacked… by himself.

Here's what happened:

Earlier that week, he reused the same password for a random website.

That website got hacked and leaked his password.

Hackers tried logging into his bank account using that leaked password.

His bank locked him out before the hackers could steal his money.

Jake had no idea that using the same password on multiple sites was dangerous. If his bank hadn't caught it in time, he could have lost everything.

1. Step One: Secure Your Passwords (No More "123456" or "password1")

Most hacks happen because people use weak or reused passwords.

Use a Password Manager

macOS already has one built-in—no need to pay for anything.

Open System Settings > Passwords.

Safari can generate and store strong passwords for you.

You can also use Bitwarden (free) or 1Password (paid) if you prefer third-party options.

💡 Quick Tip: Never use the same password for multiple accounts. If one site gets hacked, hackers will try that password on everything—email, banking, social media—and you don't want that.

2. Turn On Two-Factor Authentication (2FA) – Your Extra Layer of Security

Even if a hacker steals your password, 2FA stops them from logging in.

How to Enable 2FA on Apple ID

Open System Settings > Apple ID > Password & Security.

Turn on Two-Factor Authentication.

Now, every time you log into your Apple account on a new device, you'll get a security code on your iPhone or Mac—making it nearly impossible for hackers to break in.

💡 Also enable 2FA for your email, bank, and other important accounts.

3. Lock Down Your Mac with These Settings

Enable FileVault (Encrypts Your Data in Case of Theft)

If someone steals your Mac, FileVault ensures they can't access your files.

Open System Settings > Privacy & Security > FileVault.

Turn it ON.

Now, even if someone removes your hard drive, they won't be able to see your data without your password.

Set a Strong Mac Login Password

Your Mac shouldn't unlock with something easy like "password" or "1234."

To update your password:

Open System Settings > Users & Groups.

Click Change Password.

Set a strong, unique password.

💡 Use at least 12 characters with a mix of letters, numbers, and symbols.

Require a Password After Sleep or Screensaver

If you step away from your Mac, it should lock itself automatically.

Open System Settings > Lock Screen.

Set "Require password after sleep" to "Immediately".

Now, if someone tries to use your Mac while you're away, they'll need your password to get in.

# 4. Privacy Settings – Stop Apps from Spying on You

## Check Which Apps Have Access to Your Camera and Microphone

Open System Settings > Privacy & Security.

Click Camera and Microphone.

Disable access for apps that don't need it.

If you see something suspicious, turn it off!

## Limit Location Tracking

Many apps track your location even when they don't need to.

Open System Settings > Privacy & Security > Location Services.

Look at the apps using your location and disable unnecessary ones.

💡 Set Safari's location access to "Ask" instead of "Always"—websites don't need to know where you are all the time.

# 5. Safe Browsing: Protect Yourself from Online Scams and Trackers

## Use Safari's Built-in Privacy Features

Open Safari > Settings > Privacy.

Enable "Prevent cross-site tracking"—this stops websites from following you around.

Enable "Hide IP Address"—this prevents advertisers from tracking your location.

## Beware of Phishing Scams

If you get an email saying:

▶ "Your account is locked! Click here to reset your password!"

▶ "You've won a free iPhone!"

⚐ "Urgent: Your PayPal account is suspended!"

DON'T CLICK THE LINK.

These are phishing scams designed to steal your login info. If you're unsure, go to the website manually instead of clicking the email link.

💡 Quick Tip: If an email sounds too urgent, it's probably fake. Hackers try to scare you into making mistakes.

## 6. Public Wi-Fi Safety – Avoid Getting Hacked at Coffee Shops

Public Wi-Fi is not safe—hackers can intercept your connection and steal your data.

How to Stay Safe on Public Wi-Fi

✅ Avoid logging into banking or sensitive accounts on public networks.

✅ Use a VPN like ProtonVPN (free) to encrypt your connection.

✅ Turn off AirDrop in System Settings > General > AirDrop & Handoff to prevent strangers from sending files to you.

## Final Thoughts: Stay Smart, Stay Safe

Jake thought hacking only happened to people who clicked shady links. But he got hacked just by reusing a password.

Security isn't about paranoia—it's about being smart and making things harder for hackers.

By now, you know how to:

Use strong passwords and a password manager.

Turn on two-factor authentication for extra protection.

Lock down your Mac with FileVault and automatic lock settings.

Limit app access to your camera, microphone, and location.

Recognize phishing scams before they trick you.

Stay safe on public Wi-Fi with simple precautions.

Next up? Troubleshooting common macOS issues. Whether it's a slow Mac, Wi-Fi problems, or apps freezing, the next chapter will show you how to fix the most common Mac headaches—without calling tech support.


## Chapter 12: Advanced Tips and Hidden Features – Unlocking the Full Power of macOS

By now, you've mastered the basics of macOS, customized your system, optimized performance, and locked down security. But macOS is filled with hidden tricks and powerful features that many users—even those who have had a Mac for years—never discover.

In this chapter, we'll dive into advanced macOS tips, automation tools, and power-user tricks that can save time, boost productivity, and make using your Mac even more seamless.

Some of these features feel like magic once you start using them, and you'll wonder how you ever lived without them.

1. Mastering Spotlight – More Than Just a File Finder

Most Mac users know Spotlight as the tool for searching files, but it can do much more.

Useful Spotlight Features You May Not Know About

Perform Instant Calculations: Open Spotlight and type "250 x 8" or "$100 in euros" and get instant results.

Check the Weather: Type "weather in New York" and get an instant forecast.

Find Emails and Messages: Type someone's name to pull up recent emails or messages from them.

Convert Units on the Fly: Type "5 miles in km" or "12 ounces in grams" to get quick conversions.

Open Apps Instantly: Instead of clicking around, press Command + Spacebar, type the app name, and hit Enter.

Search the Web Faster: Type a question (like "weather in New York") and hit Enter—it opens in Safari.

Spotlight can replace your calculator, unit converter, web search bar, and even your app launcher—all without leaving your keyboard.


2. Automate Repetitive Tasks with Shortcuts and Automator

Most people manually repeat the same tasks every day without realizing macOS can automate them.

Using the Shortcuts App

Apple's Shortcuts app lets you create quick actions that automate tedious tasks.

Batch Rename Files: Select multiple files in Finder, right-click, and use Shortcuts to rename them in one click.

Auto-Resize Photos: Create a shortcut that resizes photos for social media instantly.

One-Click "Focus Mode": Set up a shortcut that closes distracting apps, opens work apps, and turns on Do Not Disturb.

Using Automator for More Powerful Workflows

Automator is macOS's built-in automation tool that can perform complex actions with one click.

Schedule Your Mac to Open Certain Apps at a Specific Time.

Automatically Sort and Move Files Based on Name or Date.

Convert Multiple Images to a Different Format at Once.

Most people never touch these tools, but they can save hours of repetitive work over time.

## 3. Universal Clipboard – Copy and Paste Across Apple Devices

If you have an iPhone or iPad, you can copy something on one device and paste it on another instantly.

How it works:

Copy text or an image on your Mac (Command + C).

Switch to your iPhone or iPad and tap Paste—it's already there.

Works the other way around too—copy something on your phone and paste it on your Mac.

No need for AirDrop, emails, or messaging yourself files—Universal Clipboard seamlessly moves text, images, and links between Apple devices.

## 4. Hidden Trackpad Gestures That Make Navigation Faster

MacBook trackpads are the best in the industry, but most users only know the basic gestures.

Here are a few hidden ones that speed up your workflow:

Three-finger swipe up – Opens Mission Control to see all open apps.

Three-finger swipe left/right – Switches between full-screen apps instantly.

Four-finger pinch – Opens Launchpad to quickly find an app.

Swipe with two fingers on Mail messages – Instantly archive or delete emails without opening them.

Tap with three fingers on a word – Instantly looks up definitions, Wikipedia entries, or translations.

Once you start using gestures, you'll spend less time clicking and more time getting things done.

5. AirDrop – The Fastest Way to Transfer Files Between Apple Devices

Forget email, USB drives, or cloud uploads—AirDrop is the best way to transfer files between Macs, iPhones, and iPads.

Send photos, documents, and links instantly between Apple devices.

No internet required—works over Bluetooth and Wi-Fi.

Preserves quality—photos and videos don't get compressed like when sent through messaging apps.

To use AirDrop:

Open Finder and click AirDrop in the sidebar.

Make sure the receiving device has AirDrop enabled in System Settings.

Drag and drop the file onto the recipient's icon.

It's fast, reliable, and seamless—and once you get used to it, you'll never go back to emailing files to yourself.

6. Terminal Commands for Power Users (Simple But Powerful)

Most Mac users never open Terminal, but knowing a few basic commands can help you unlock hidden macOS features.

Useful Terminal Commands Anyone Can Use

Show Hidden Files and Folders:

defaults write com.apple.Finder AppleShowAllFiles true; killall Finder

Speed Up Window Animations:

defaults write NSGlobalDomain NSAutomaticWindowAnimationsEnabled -bool false

Flush DNS Cache (Fixes Some Internet Issues):

sudo dscacheutil -flushcache; sudo killall -HUP mDNSResponder

Prevent Your Mac from Sleeping Until You Say So:

caffeinate -u -t 3600 (Keeps it awake for 1 hour)

Terminal is powerful, but it's also easy to break things if you don't know what you're doing. If in doubt, stick with graphical settings.

7. Virtual Desktops (Spaces) – Stay Organized While Multitasking

If your screen is always cluttered with too many open apps, Spaces (virtual desktops) can help.

Swipe up with three fingers to open Mission Control.

Drag an app to the top of the screen to create a new desktop space.

Swipe left/right with three fingers to switch between desktops instantly.

Use Spaces to separate work, entertainment, and communication apps, so you're not constantly minimizing and reopening windows.

Final Thoughts: You're Now a macOS Power User

At the start of this book, you might have been just getting familiar with macOS. Now, you know:

Spotlight can replace your calculator, app launcher, and search bar.

Shortcuts and Automator can eliminate repetitive tasks.

Universal Clipboard makes working between devices seamless.

AirDrop is the fastest way to move files between Apple devices.

Terminal unlocks hidden settings for power users.

Virtual desktops (Spaces) help organize your workflow.

By mastering these tools, you're no longer just using your Mac—you're making it work for you.

In the final chapter, we'll cover how to keep learning and stay updated so your macOS skills never fall behind. Get ready to take your Mac skills to the next level!


Final Chapter: Taking Your macOS Knowledge to the Next Level

You've come a long way.

At the beginning of this book, you might have felt a little lost—maybe switching from Windows, or maybe just trying to figure out what makes macOS different. Now, you understand your Mac inside and out.

You know how to customize it, troubleshoot issues, optimize performance, and even use hidden features that many Mac users never discover.

But technology is always evolving, and staying up to date with macOS is just as important as learning the basics. This final chapter will show you where to keep learning, how to stay informed about updates, and where to get help if you ever run into problems.

# 1. Where to Learn More About macOS

Even though you now have a solid foundation, there's always more to learn.

## Apple's Official Support Resources

Mac User Guide: Apple's official guide covers every feature of macOS.

Mac Tips and Tricks: Apple occasionally updates its Tips app, which you can find in Launchpad.

## Online Communities and Forums

Sometimes, the best way to learn is from other Mac users.

r/macOS on Reddit – A great place to discuss macOS, ask for advice, and see what other users are doing.

Apple Discussions – Apple's own forums where users share fixes and tips.

MacRumors Forums – A great resource for discussions on macOS updates and troubleshooting.

# 2. Keeping Your Mac Updated (Without Surprises)

## How to Stay on Top of macOS Updates

macOS gets major updates once a year, usually in the fall. Smaller updates with bug fixes and security patches come throughout the year.

To check for updates, go to System Settings > General > Software Update.

Turn on Automatic Updates, but consider setting it to "Notify Me" instead of "Install Automatically" so you can review changes first.

## Should You Update Right Away?

New macOS versions sometimes introduce bugs. If you rely on your Mac for work, wait a week or two before updating—this gives Apple time to fix any early issues.

3. When to Get Help (And Where to Find It)

Even experienced Mac users run into problems from time to time. Here's how to know when you need outside help—and where to find it.

Fix It Yourself First

Before seeking help, try these steps:

Restart your Mac (fixes many minor issues).

Check online forums—someone else has probably had the same problem.

Search Apple's Support Pages for step-by-step guides.

If You Need Professional Support

If your Mac is experiencing hardware issues, won't turn on, or has a persistent software problem, it might be time to contact Apple.

Apple Support (Online or Phone) – Visit to chat or schedule a call.

Apple Stores and Authorized Repair Shops – If you're near an Apple Store, you can book a Genius Bar appointment.

💡 Tip: If your Mac is under AppleCare+, repairs may be free or significantly discounted.

Final Thoughts: You're Now a Confident Mac User

At the start of this journey, you may have been just learning the basics. Now, you know how to:

Navigate macOS with ease.

Customize your Mac to fit your needs.

Fix common problems yourself.

Keep your Mac running efficiently.

Protect your privacy and security.

Unlock advanced features that most users never use.

The best part? This is just the beginning. The more you use your Mac, the more comfortable and efficient you'll become.

So go ahead—explore, experiment, and enjoy your Mac to the fullest.

Your Mac is no longer just a computer. It's a tool that works for you.

Happy computing!

## Glossary – Understanding macOS Terminology

AirDrop

A feature that allows wireless file sharing between Apple devices using Bluetooth and Wi-Fi.

Apple ID

The account used to access iCloud, the App Store, FaceTime, iMessage, and other Apple services.

Command (⌘) Key

The main keyboard shortcut key in macOS, similar to the Ctrl key in Windows.

Control Center

A panel that provides quick access to Wi-Fi, Bluetooth, brightness, sound, and other system controls.

Dock

The macOS application launcher at the bottom of the screen, used to open and switch between apps.

Finder

The macOS file management system, similar to File Explorer on Windows.

FileVault

Apple's built-in encryption system that protects all files on your Mac.

Force Quit

A method for closing frozen or unresponsive apps using Command (⌘) + Option + Esc.

Gatekeeper

A security feature in macOS that prevents unauthorized apps from running unless they are from the App Store or an identified developer.

Gestures

Multi-touch trackpad shortcuts that allow users to navigate macOS with swipes, pinches, and taps.

Launchpad

A full-screen grid of applications, similar to the app drawer on an iPhone or iPad.

Mac App Store

The official marketplace for downloading and updating macOS applications.

Mission Control

A macOS feature that displays all open windows, full-screen apps, and virtual desktops for easy multitasking.

Spotlight Search

The system-wide search tool used to quickly find files, apps, and even perform calculations or web searches using Command (⌘) + Spacebar.

Terminal

The command-line interface for macOS, used for executing advanced system commands.

Time Machine

Apple's built-in backup system that automatically saves copies of files and system data.

Trackpad Gestures

Swipes and pinches that allow users to navigate macOS more efficiently.

Virtual Desktops (Spaces)

Multiple desktops that help organize open apps and tasks, accessed via Mission Control.

## Quick Reference Guide – Essential macOS Shortcuts & Tips

Common Keyboard Shortcuts

Finder Tips

Show/Hide Hidden Files:

Press Command (⌘) + Shift + . to toggle the visibility of hidden files in Finder.

Quick Look:

Select a file and press Spacebar to preview it without opening it.

Create New Folder:

Press Command (⌘) + Shift + N to create a new folder in Finder.

Search in Finder:

Press Command (⌘) + F to search within Finder, and use filters like file type and date modified.

Mission Control and Spaces

Mission Control (Show All Open Windows):

Swipe up with three fingers (trackpad) or press F3 on your keyboard.

Switch Between Desktops:

Swipe left or right with three fingers (trackpad) to switch between virtual desktops (Spaces).

Move a Window to Another Desktop:

Open Mission Control, then drag the window to the desired desktop at the top of the screen.

Trackpad Gestures

Two-Finger Scroll:

Scroll up or down using two fingers on the trackpad.

Pinch to Zoom:

Use two fingers to pinch and zoom in or out, similar to touchscreens.

Three-Finger Swipe Up:

Opens Mission Control, showing all open windows.

Three-Finger Swipe Left/Right:

Switch between full-screen apps.

Four-Finger Pinch:

Opens Launchpad, showing all installed applications.

File and App Management

Quickly Close a Window:

Press Command (⌘) + W to close the current window.

Quit an App:

Press Command (⌘) + Q to quit the currently active app.

Force Quit an App:

If an app is frozen, press Command (⌘) + Option + Esc, select the app, and click Force Quit.

Switch Between Open Apps:

Press Command (⌘) + Tab to cycle through open apps.

Minimize a Window:

Press Command (⌘) + M to minimize the active window.

System Settings Shortcuts

Open System Settings:

Click the Apple logo (top left) > System Settings, or press Command (⌘) + Spacebar, then type System Settings in Spotlight.

Change Display Brightness:

Use the F1 and F2 keys to decrease or increase the brightness.

Open Siri:

Click the Siri icon in the menu bar or press Command (⌘) + Spacebar and say "Hey Siri."

Safari Tips

Open a New Tab:

Press Command (⌘) + T to open a new tab in Safari.

Reopen a Closed Tab:

Press Command (⌘) + Shift + T to reopen your last closed tab.

Private Browsing:

Press Command (⌘) + Shift + N to open a private browsing window.

Clear Browsing History:

Press Command (⌘) + Shift + Delete to clear your browsing history.

Quick Time Tips

Record Screen:

Open QuickTime Player, click File > New Screen Recording, and click the red button to start recording.

Record Audio:

Open QuickTime Player, click File > New Audio Recording, and press the red button to start recording.

System Maintenance

Free Up Storage:

 Go to System Settings > General > Storage and click Review Files to remove large files and apps you don't need.

Check for Updates:

 Open System Settings > General > Software Update to check for and install any macOS updates.

Reboot Your Mac:

 Regularly restart your Mac to keep it running efficiently.

Essential Apps to Consider

LibreOffice:

 A free alternative to Microsoft Office, compatible with Word, Excel, and PowerPoint.

GIMP:

 A free image editor that is a great alternative to Photoshop.

DaVinci Resolve:

 A powerful free video editing tool.

1Password:

 A password manager that helps securely store and manage all your passwords.

## About the Author

Ryan Nowack is a technology writer and IT professional with extensive experience in macOS, IT support, and troubleshooting. With a passion for simplifying technology for everyday users, Ryan has spent years helping individuals and businesses optimize their systems and resolve technical issues.

Ryan's career has focused on hardware, software, networking, and security, giving him a well-rounded understanding of the tech world. He is dedicated to breaking down complex tech topics into easy-to-understand, practical guides that empower users to make the most out of their devices.

When he's not writing, Ryan enjoys experimenting with new technology, learning about self-sufficient tech setups, and exploring creative software tools. His goal is to help people use technology efficiently and confidently, without the frustration that often comes with learning new systems.

Ryan's expertise and approachable writing style have made him a go-to resource for beginners looking to master their tech.